RELIGIONS OF THE WORLD

I Am
Jewish

❦ BERNARD P. WEISS ❦

The Rosen Publishing Group's
PowerKids Press
New York

Published in 1996, 2003 by The Rosen Publishing Group, Inc.
29 East 21st Street, New York, NY 10010

Revised Edition 2003

Editor: Gillian Houghton
Book Design: Erin McKenna and Kim Sonsky
Text Revisions: Jennifer Way

Photo credits: Cover photo © Peter Turnley/Corbis; p. 4 © Bobbe Wolf/International Stock; p. 7, 16, 19 © Bill Aron; p. 8 © V. Shone/Gamma Liaison; p. 11 © George Ancona/International Stock; pp. 12, 15 courtesy of the Dizengoff family; p. 20 © E. Baitel/Gamma Liaison.

Weiss, Bernard P.
     I am Jewish / Bernard P. Weiss.
        p.   cm.—(Religions of the world)
     Includes index.
     Summary: Introduces the ancient religion of Judaism through the eyes of a Jewish child living in St. Louis.
     ISBN 0-8239-6810-3
     1. Judaism—juvenile literature. [I. Judaism.] I. Title. II. Series: Religions of the world (Rosen Publishing Group)
     BM573.W45 1996
     296—dc20   96-733

Manufactured in the United States of America

Contents

Being Jewish

My name is David. I live in St. Louis, Missouri. I am Jewish. There are three major kinds of Judaism today. They are Reform, Conservative, and Orthodox Judaism. Reform Judaism is the least strict, and Orthodox Judaism is very traditional. Conservative Judaism is somewhere between the two.

The first Jew was a man named Abraham. Jews believe that Abraham made an agreement with God, promising to follow the Jewish law. In return, God blessed Abraham, his children, and all of his **descendants**.

◄ *Jews follow the laws of their faith. Many families keep kosher, meaning they prepare and keep food according to Jewish law.*

The Sabbath

The Ten Commandments make up part of the Jewish law. Keeping the Sabbath is one of the Ten Commandments. The Sabbath is a day of worship that begins every Friday at sundown and that ends at sundown on Saturday.

The Sabbath celebrates the seventh day of Creation. The seventh day is the day on which God rested after making the world. We do not work on the Sabbath. Meals are prepared ahead of time so that we do not have to cook on the Sabbath. On the Sabbath, we attend services and spend time with our families.

The Sabbath celebration begins with the lighting of two candles. One candle stands for remembrance of the Sabbath, and the other candle stands for observance. ▶

Synagogue

On the Sabbath, my family says special prayers. We go to a **synagogue**. The synagogue is a house of prayer. When my father prays, he wears a **talit**, or prayer shawl. Men and boys cover their heads with small caps called **yarmulkes**.

A rabbi leads the Sabbath service with the help of a cantor. The rabbi is a religious guide and teacher who helps us to think about problems in life. The cantor chants traditional Jewish songs and leads us in prayer.

◀ *A synagogue is a Jewish house of prayer and study. It is a place for the Jewish community to come together.*

The Hebrew Bible

At the synagogue, the rabbi reads from the Torah. Torah is the Hebrew name for the first five books of the Hebrew Bible. Christians might know the Hebrew Bible as the Old Testament. The Torah was written long ago in Hebrew, the language of the Jews. The Torah is a record of Jewish history, Jewish law, and Jewish belief.

In Hebrew, my name looks like this:

דָּוִד

I cannot read Hebrew yet, but I will learn when I am older.

The Torah is so holy that no one is allowed to touch the paper on which it is written. ▶

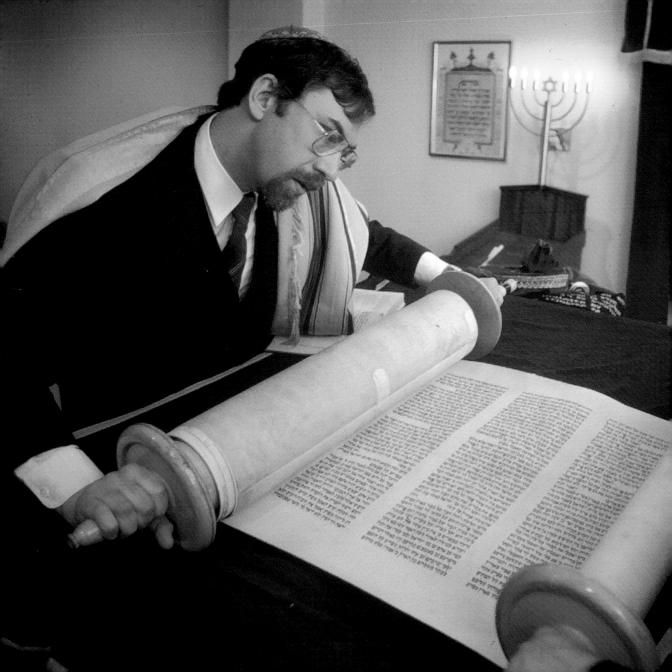

Bar Mitzvah

When I turn 13, I will have a **bar mitzvah**. The bar mitzvah is a traditional ceremony. Before my bar mitzvah, I will learn to read and speak Hebrew. I will read from the Torah in front of everyone in the synagogue. This reading shows that I am an adult, ready to share the responsibilities of Jewish life. Then we will have a reception to celebrate.

When my younger sister turns 12, she will have a **bat mitzvah**. She will also read from the Torah and celebrate her entry into adult Jewish life.

◄ Once a boy has had his bar mitzvah, he is considered an adult and can participate in religious services.

Marriage

My eldest sister is getting married soon. My father says that marriage is one of the most sacred, or holy, events in Jewish life. It is a new beginning for the bride and groom. They will be married under a wedding canopy called a **chuppah**. Our rabbi will perform the wedding. At the end of the ceremony, the groom will break a glass by stepping on it, and everyone will shout *Mazel tov!* which means "congratulations." Then we will celebrate with a festive meal and a party.

In a Jewish wedding, the bride and groom are married under a chuppah, representing the home that the bride and groom will share. ▶

The High Holy Days

Rosh Hashanah and Yom Kippur are called the High Holy Days. We spend these days at the synagogue and read from special prayer books. Rosh Hashanah is the Jewish New Year. It occurs every fall. On Rosh Hashanah, we eat apples dipped in honey, representing our hopes for a sweet new year. Nine days after Rosh Hashanah, we celebrate Yom Kippur. On Yom Kippur, we ask God to forgive us for the bad things we have done in the past year. We fast on Yom Kippur. This means that we do not eat or drink anything.

◀ *To indicate the beginning and end of the High Holy Days, the rabbi blows a special horn called a shofar.*

Passover

My favorite holiday is Passover. My family and our friends gather for a meal called a **seder**. At the seder, we read from the **Haggadah**. This book tells how the Jews, led by Moses, escaped from slavery in Egypt. A place at the Passover table is set for Elijah, the **prophet** whose appearance is believed to lead to the coming of the **Messiah**, the being who we believe will bring peace on Earth.

During Passover, we do not eat any foods, such as bread, that are made with yeast. This is to remind us that, when the Jews fled Egypt, they did not have time to bake bread.

Special foods are eaten at the Passover seder, such as parsley, bitter herbs, apples, and gefilte fish. ▶

Jerusalem

Many Jews live in Israel. Israel is a country in the Middle East. In Israel, many people speak Hebrew. Jerusalem is the most holy city in Israel. It is the city in which the First Temple was built. The First Temple was destroyed in one of many wars in Jerusalem. The Second Temple was built and later was destroyed. If you go to Jerusalem today, you can still see the remaining wall from the Second Temple. It is called the Western, or the Wailing, Wall. Many Jews go there to pray. I hope to pray at the Wailing Wall some day.

◀ *Jews from all over the world go to the Wailing Wall in Jerusalem to pray.*

Hanukkah

According to Jewish belief, a sacred lamp always burned in the Temple in Jerusalem. More than 2,000 years ago, the Temple was taken over by enemies of the Jews. When the Jews won back the Temple, they had only enough sacred oil to burn the lamp for one night. Amazingly, the lamp burned for eight days and nights, just long enough to prepare more oil! Hanukkah is a celebration of this miracle of light. During each night of Hanukkah, also known as the Festival of Lights, we light a candle on the **menorah**.

Glossary

bar/bat mitzvah (BAR/BOT MITS-vah) A service held in honor of a Jewish youth becoming an adult.

chuppah (HUH-pah) A covering over the bride and groom during a wedding.

descendants (dih-SEN-dents) People born of a certain family or group.

Haggadah (heh-GAH-dah) A book that tells the story of the Jews leaving Egypt.

menorah (meh-NOR-uh) A candleholder with seven or nine candles, used in Jewish worship.

Messiah (meh-SY-uh) The expected king of the Jews.

prophet (PRAH-fet) One who tells the future.

seder (SAY-dur) A meal eaten in honor of Passover.

synagogue (SIH-nih-gog) A temple or a house of prayer.

talit (ta-LEET) Prayer shawl.

yarmulkes (YAH-mah-kos) Head coverings.

Index

Web Sites

Due to the changing nature of Internet links, PowerKids Press has developed an online list of Web sites related to the subject of this book. This site is updated regularly. Please use this link to access the list:

www.powerkidslinks.com/rotw/jewish/